I'M OKAY

Written by

Vidah Ryan

Illustrations by Theresa Stites

Copyright © 2024 by Vidah Ryan Ventures Ltd.

All rights reserved. No part of this book may be reproduced or used in any manner without written permission of the copyright owner except for the use of quotations in a book review.

ISBN # 9798878089418

DEDICATION

To our son, Ryan Glenn – we miss you!

You taught us so much in your short life:

- Your big brother (Kuya) lives everyday with adventure and commitment to his family, friends, and wife. His new married life adventure has just begun.
- Your big sister (Ate) loves with her whole heart and gives nothing less than 100% to everyone lucky enough to know her.
- Your little sister (Ash) pushes herself to be better every day, knowing you will always be her #1 cheerleader in life.
- Your family (Lolo, Lola, Tita's, Tito's, Lola M) and friends remember and cherish their memories of you.

Your Dad and I remember your bravery and how hard you fought to be with us as long as you could. We try to be brave in a life without you and try every day to remember the moments you honored us with. We make new memories the way we know you would have wanted us to.

This is your story and your legacy. We will forever love you!

4

ACKNOWLEDGEMENTS

To my friend Dawn:

You left this world too soon, but this book is the result of my friendship with you.

At my time of grief, you encouraged me to write. All the words that I couldn't express verbally to anyone were captured in my writing. You were the only one I could trust to read those words, without judgement. You instinctively knew all I needed was someone to cry and feel my pain through my writing.

I remember us sitting on the park bench as you read my journals and we spent hours crying afterward. Then in time, you encouraged me to write a book to help others through their grief.

If this book helps even one mother through her grief or one sibling through their pain – our shared tears will have been worthwhile.

You learned to walk and had the biggest smile.

You saw the Christmas tree and tried to run for the very first time.

You fell on the carpet floor.

Your smile went away, and you started to cry.

I whispered in your ear, as I held you in my arms:

I FEEL YOU

I HEAR YOU

I LOVE YOU – YOU'RE OKAY!

You learned to rollerblade with your brother and had the biggest smile.

As you got faster, you fell over a small stone.

Your smile went away, and you started to cry.

I whispered in your ear, as I held you in my arms:

I FEEL YOU

I HEAR YOU

I LOVE YOU – YOU'RE OKAY!

You learned to ride a bike with your big sister and had the biggest smile.

As you went down a tall hill, you fell but got up quickly.

Your smile went away, and you started to cry.

I whispered in your ear, as I held you in my arms:

I FEEL YOU

I HEAR YOU

I LOVE YOU – YOU'RE OKAY!

You learned to do a cartwheel with your little sister and had the biggest smile.

You landed hard on the sidewalk, but you didn't cry.

There were tears in my eyes.

I whispered in your ear, as I gave you a hug:

I FEEL YOU

I HEAR YOU

I LOVE YOU – YOU'RE OKAY!

You learned to play games with your brother and sisters and always had the biggest smile.

I watched you play with them and saw the joy on your face.

You hated to lose a game, but you didn't cry.

There were tears in my eyes.

I whispered in your ear, as I gave you a hug:

I FEEL YOU

I HEAR YOU

I LOVE YOU – YOU'RE OKAY!

You got sick but you still smiled.

You were so brave as you laid on the hospital bed.

There were tears in your eyes.

I whispered in your ear, as I gave you a hug:

I FEEL YOU

I HEAR YOU

I LOVE YOU – YOU'RE OKAY!

You learned to play on your own.

Building blocks were your favorite toys.

You couldn't play outside with your friends or your brother and sisters.

There were tears in my eyes.

I whispered in your ear, as I gave you a hug:

I FEEL YOU

I HEAR YOU

I LOVE YOU – YOU'RE OKAY!

We had to say goodbye to you.

Our smiles went away, and we started to cry.

There were tears in our eyes.

I whispered to myself:

I DON'T FEEL YOU

I DON'T HEAR YOU

I LOVE YOU – IT'S NOT OKAY!

Years later, your brother and sisters learned to play

games by the campfire with the biggest smiles again.

They would remember playing with you and they didn't cry.

There were tears in my eyes.

I whispered to myself:

I'M STARTING TO FEEL YOU

I'M STARTING TO HEAR YOU

I LOVE YOU – IT'S STARTING TO BE OKAY!

Your brother got married today to the most beautiful bride and had the biggest smile.

Your sisters were there with tears in their eyes.

I whispered to myself:

I FEEL YOU NOW

I HEAR YOU NOW

I LOVE YOU – I'M OKAY!

ABOUT THE AUTHOR

I am a mother of 4 children – 3 are now grown adults and the other is our son who we lost at the young age of 9 years old. This is when my journey as a writer began.

My career has been in customer leadership roles, and I've recently prioritized my passion for writing.

I would be honored if you followed my writing or shared your experiences on grief or loss:

      Website: www.vidahryan.com

      Email: vidahryang@gmail.com

Memories remind us of the beautiful moments

when our children are little.

32

Memories remind us of how our children learn and grow everyday.

Memories remind us of all the amazing moments we share with our children.